How to Fix the Future

Using Cooperative Economics

How to Fix the Future

Using Cooperative Economics

Mark A. Young

Copyright © 2012, Mark A. Young

All rights reserved. No part of this book may be reproduced, stored, or transmitted by any means—whether auditory, graphic, mechanical, or electronic—without written permission of both publisher and author, except in the case of brief excerpts used in critical articles and reviews. Unauthorized reproduction of any part of this work is illegal and is punishable by law.

ISBN 978-1-300-09647-4

Contents

Introduction vii

Chapter 1: What Is Cooperative Economics? 1

Chapter 2: What Is Fiat Money? 5

Chapter 3: Super Macroeconomics 11

Chapter 4: The Myth of Scarcity 21

Chapter 5: Private Money for Public Uses 23

Chapter 6: A Global Cooperative Economic System 31

Chapter 7: Basic Market Principles 39

Chapter 8: The Benefits of a Cooperative Economic System 45

Chapter 9: The Impacts of a Cooperative Economic System 55

Chapter 10: The Big Transition 59

Introduction

If you watch the news on any day of the week, it's easy to see that the world is plagued with war, failed states, disease, poverty, environmental contamination and destruction, drought, starvation, and ethnic unrest, to name just a few. On a national level, we are and have been experiencing problems concerning economic disparity, crime, unemployment, budget deficits, healthcare, decaying cities, youth violence, industry downsizing, homelessness, the failure of our schools, and many more.

Although these are an array of problems that cover many aspects of our world and society, in general they all have a common factor. That factor is money, the lust for money, or the lack of money. These problems arise from an indirect effect of not having enough money, the outcome of people trying to gain more money, or the result of the difference in the amount of money certain groups have. Money, resources, wealth, or whatever you want to call it, in some way drives the natural competition and conflict inherent in our global economy that allows the rich to get richer, the poor to get poorer, and the middle class to shrink in a spiral toward economic unsustainability.

A question that I often ask people is: why are some people rich and some people poor? The answers are common, most people answer that it is just the way things are, always will be, or that some people work harder, or are smarter, more blessed, luckier, etc. You have to start at 50,000 feet in the super macroeconomic level and take more in-depth examination of the world's monetary system structure to see that although this is the way things are now, it most certainly does not have to remain this way.

A comprehensive knowledge of our present system is essential to understanding why and how all these problems exist, are interrelated, and how to eliminate the vast majority of them. One analogy that often helps in understanding how our current system works is to compare the monetary system to a monopoly game; the players are the world's richest companies, industrialized nations, persons, and international banks. In a closed monetary system, they have made the rules of the game; they control the bank, and dictate how much money is in the bank. We the people, in countries all over the world, are the pawns of the game. These rules, created and established for the rest of us, affect how we live, learn, grow, and die.

It may not be quite that dramatic, but under the current rules, the amount of wealth a government or country possesses comes directly from the wealth of its industries and citizens through taxation or through a governments' direct ownership of industries. Generating revenue in this way puts unnecessary limits on the wealth of individuals, nations, and the world as a whole. If a country, state, city, or neighborhood has no industry or wealthy people, then it has no wealth. This causes countries to be rich or poor and creates an imbalance that causes people to be rich or poor. This imbalance directly and indirectly causes problems that correlate with a lust for or lack of money. The system is like a game and we must change the rules of the game to create a more equal, prosperous, fair, and progressive world.

This book studies the merits of restructuring our current global monetary system into a model that will allow nations to create a fundamentally limitless supply of money (fiat money) and eliminate the need for taxation or public ownership of private property to raise revenue. Many people with whom I have spoken on this topic dismiss the creation of a fiat money system as far too abstract, not worth serious examination, or not at all possible. In this book, I will demonstrate how it works.

Critics will say it is not feasible because allowing unlimited fiat money would collapse the economy, cause uncontrollable inflation, or that it is just not possible to create money out of thin air. I am here to tell you that it is indeed possible to eliminate taxation and still provide for the common good. It is possible to create money out of thin air. It happens all the time.

The world's long-term outlook says that we cannot afford *not* to change how our monetary system operates. One reason that so many people are detached from politics and leaders is that our current system is lacking faith in tomorrow and a positive outlook on the future. Each solution seems to be more of the same depending on who is in power but nothing ever substantially changes within the masses for the better.

The issues of wealth and the economy play such an important role in people's lives today. We can no longer take it for granted that we can solve our problems using the same solutions that we have employed over the last thirty years. The arguments are few and are either very similar or are not practical to today's society. Changes involving the political dogma of adjusting interest rates, taxation rates, social spending, trade policies, and regulations are simply not enough to address the level of problems and inequalities present today. Most socialist theories, calling for a basic redistribution of wealth through increased taxation, are not popular enough with the masses of people in many countries making change improbable. Socialism penalizes a class of society that most of us aspire to be in, and can be a detriment to business, making it an illogical option and not possible on a global scale because the same wealth imbalances will still exist.

According to the Organization for Economic Cooperation and Development, over the past thirty years, inequality in Sweden, Germany, Israel, Finland, and New Zealand has grown as fast as or faster than inequality in the United States. Inequality is also on the rise and one of the main threats to the stability of developing nations such as China, India, and Brazil. Global problems require global solutions.

Solutions to our economic problems exist within both the capitalistic systems we've created and the technological advances made over the past decades. The ability for us to change the economic and monetary structure has always existed but has only been optimal since the onset of the information age. We can enhance the capitalistic infrastructure that currently exists worldwide and allow it to operate at its highest level without causing the suffering and inequality currently associated with it. We have to begin by asking the question, "What if?" Then think about our economic and monetary system exactly as it is, a game, a game that we can control, and not a game that controls us. We must find a way to utilize the best aspects of capitalism and provide the support and safety nets that a purely capitalistic society cannot.

The question of what would happen if there were no more taxes provides the framework to solve these problems. Obviously many companies and individuals would have a lot more money to expend and or save. Other businesses and individuals that have government contracts or employment would suffer. What would we do about healthcare, social security, education, or any of the other thousands of governmental functions that would cease? Instead of taxation, what if we allow governments to create their own fiat revenue. This revenue could replace the missing revenue from taxation. What if all the other nations in the world adopt the same restructuring and we forgave all national debts or paid them off with fiat revenues? Politicians, scholars, and planners can create budgets separate from the monetary system of capitalism. Under this system, every nation could raise the minimum wage to a standard of living where everyone could afford decent shelter and modern conveniences. Universities and schools can be free and operate at full capacity. There could always be 100 percent employment through government projects, if necessary. Would these changes destabilize the world economy, or could we implement them within the current system, without collapse, to usher in a new civilization?

The following pages will answer these questions and map out solutions to the problems described. For the purposes of this book, I will call this system *Cooperative Economics*. It creates monetary cooperation between existing capitalism and the governmental systems that exist today and it pulls from the best aspects of each to create a sustainable system in order to fix the future.

Chapter One

What is Cooperative Economics?

In the simplest terms *Cooperative Economics*, as defined is this book, is the restructuring of the current monetary system to allow the creation of fiat money by nations, and the elimination of the need for taxation. This would eliminate a government's dependence on the capitalistic system by allowing it to create its own revenue through fiat, and it would eliminate the burden of taxes. While this may not sound like a solution to many of the world's problems, in reality, it can provide the framework and opportunity to do great things in society. It can allow us to reach our full potential as a global community, which would spur growth, give countries the ability to correct longstanding economic disparities, and provide a modern standard of living to the world's citizens. It would also give people the ability for gainful employment and prosperity.

Why do we need a change in how our monetary system operates? Because change is inevitable and history teaches us that all major systems evolve and change over time. For instance, we once lived in an agricultural society and moved to an industrial society. Now we live in a society of information technology. The same is true for transportation, from horseback to planes and automobiles, and manual assembly to automation, and snail mail to email. The list goes on, but in the case of our monetary system, there has not been a substantive change for centuries. In the United States, there has been a Central Bank since 1913 with no major changes beyond the removal of the gold standard. The monetary and central banking systems (central banks are private institutions that manage a nation state's currency, money supply, and interest rates) in the world have not evolved to keep pace with the changing dynamics, technologies, and needs of today's society. It has actually been a hindrance to the much-needed progress on a macro scale.

Returning to sovereign national governments the ability and the right to create monetary resources or fiat money as needed, rights currently held and manipulated by privately owned central banks, reverses the present system of requiring a nation's revenues to come from its industries and citizens through taxation. This ability would give nations, businesses, and industries the power to eliminate poverty and unemployment by removing the limitation of investing into and creating new industries and infrastructure. This means that governments would not have to depend on taxes for revenue. They would have the ability to fund any project, issue, industry, or program, as desired, without limitation. Nations, businesses, and industries around the world would immediately have the ability to fund the creation of new businesses and expand existing businesses; build irrigation systems, housing, and infrastructure; create jobs; and spur economic growth.

The creation of a *Global Fiat Monetary System* represents the reorganizing of the current system to allow nations to establish a fiat money supply based on agreed methodologies. These methodologies will be discussed later but incorporate a nation's population, capitalistic infrastructure, and various aspects of a country's level of development. This will ultimately allow countries to create fiat revenues based on periodic budgets that incorporate planned expenditures based first on the revenue lost from the elimination of taxation and second on the cost of new spending associated with improving and regulating economies, building infrastructure, and ensuring 100 percent employment.

There are several reasons why Cooperative Economics is a viable alternative to restructure our current global monetary system using our existing capitalistic infrastructure, the platform of the United Nations, and existing democratic processes. One, Cooperative Economics would benefit all segments of society: rich, poor, and the middle class in all participating nations. Two, by depending on the current capitalistic infrastructure, existing industries, businesses, banks, and companies of all kinds would continue to exist and would receive the benefits associated with Cooperative Economics through the elimination of taxes, increased disposable income by the populations, and spurred economic growth. Three, Cooperative Economics can occur within the framework of existing laws and legislative processes. Four, governments can implement Cooperative Economics quickly because it does not change the existing infrastructure, which makes for a bloodless and relatively pleasant revolution. The only thing required is a change in the perspective of how we view the creation and purpose of money, along with the ability to think outside the box.

Chapter Two

What Is Fiat Money?

A simple definition of fiat money is the creation of a money supply by decree by either a sovereign nation or a central bank. In reality it is the money you receive when you purchase a home or open a business or enter into a debt agreement with a lender. It is money not backed by any precious metal and exists because a government says it does.

The question is who creates fiat money, why, and under what circumstances. Article I, Section 8 of the U.S. Constitution gives Congress the power to coin money, regulate the value thereof, and of foreign coin, as well as fix the standard of weights and measures.

There are essentially two ways to view the creation of fiat money. The first is within the previous definition, which alludes to the value of the fiat money without precious metals to back it up, and the value of money managed in the abstract by central banks. An example of this is the ever-decreasing purchasing power of the dollar and the ever-present compensation for inflation. Consider what a dollar would have been worth in 1970. This fiat money comes mainly from our fractional reserve system, which allows banks to create money out of thin air.

For example, if a bank has $100 million in deposits, our monetary policies allow that bank to loan out well over the $100 million it actually has on deposit. So if this bank loans out $150 million or $50 million more than what it has on deposit, it has created $50 million in fiat money. This occurs when the borrower spends it and pays it back with interest. There are many positive and negative aspects associated with the practice. One, it allows for the growth of the economy beyond what would be possible if the value of money were only backed by a precious metal like gold. On the other hand, it also causes instability that creates bubbles that can burst and lead to inflation in the economy.

The second negative possibility is much smaller in proportion and concerns the practice of the central banks being the lender of last resort, and the printing and issuing of debt and credit. Modern central banks don't have to print bills to create new money; they just add money to their customers' checking accounts because their customers are mainly banks and national governments. Think of the process as a national accounting system managed and controlled by the Central Bank, where to create money all that has to done is to increase the amount of debt and receivables on a balance sheet.

During the recent debt debate in Congress, an economics professor suggested a jumbo coin solution. Under this scenario, the Treasury, which issues any value of coin under our agreement with the Federal Reserve, would issue a two trillion dollar coin and deposit it in the account of the U.S. government to ensure that there would be no default on the debt. If this is possible, then what else could we accomplish, if we change the rules of the system? There is talk about returning the monetary system to a gold standard. However, every time a person is born, more resources and capital are needed in the system to support that new person. Under the gold standard, there would be less capital every time a person is born, thereby causing deflation of the economy and lower wages. The standard itself would have to be devalued to account for an increased need for capital, unless mining gold forever were an option. Devaluing the value of gold to keep up with the capital needs of a nation defeats the purpose of having a gold standard in the first place.

I would agree that many policies of the Federal Reserve and other central banks do cause inflation and instability in our economics system. However, I disagree on the current popular solution, which is to reduce the printing of money. This would only lead to decrease in the money supply. I propose increasing the money supply, but under a different monetary structure.

Money, capital, wealth, or whatever you would like to call it, needs to be elastic and able to expand when needed and contract when needed. The best factor for predicting that need accurately is population, not gold or some precious metal, not our fractional reserve system, and not any central banking monetary policy adjustments. Thomas Jefferson once said that, "If the American people ever allow private banks to control the issuance of their currency, first by inflation and then by deflation, the banks and corporations that will grow up around them will deprive the people of all their property until their children will wake up homeless on the continent their fathers conquered." Nations and governments must begin to consider moving from a tax-based revenue system to a fiat-based revenue system, and allowing the capitalistic system to exist separately but in conjunction with the fiat system.

I will explain how this is done structurally in a later chapter, but understanding this concept will be key to understanding Cooperative Economics. How can you create money out of thin air? In short, governments create money the same way central banks do it now and by the power vested in sovereign nations. Article I, Section 8 of the Constitution of the United States of America gives my government the explicit power to create money.

The history of fiat money created by individual governments is not new and has occurred many times throughout history, usually not with good consequences. Documented from 900 AD in China to the 1920s in Germany, most of these instances involved troubled economies short on the supply of money and burdened with debt. The reasons these systems failed were three-fold. First, they were not global systems but they operated in the vacuums of their own countries. Second, these countries never established a constant formula for the creation of fiat money that balanced its economic production with the need for gap financing to support the economy and its citizens. This in turn always led to inflation and a devaluation of the fiat money created. Third, these countries tried to combine the creation of fiat money, debt issuance, and taxation instead of viewing the creation of fiat money as a single source of government revenue and the elimination of debt and taxation altogether.

Chapter Three

Super Macroeconomics

Super Macroeconomics means searching for solutions and viewing economics from outside the current system and changing the rules of the monetary system and capitalistic game that we play for the benefit of all people. It is unlike macroeconomics, which views economics and monetary policy from inside the current box using two hundred years of economic dogma and seeks solutions from inside the same box. Super Macroeconomics applies to how we could design a just system that incorporates the best of all worlds and utilizes what we have learned about human nature, capitalism, and our goals to create a better world.

Socialism, Communism, and Capitalism

The big three "isms" that have controlled our economic futures over the past several centuries are still around, but they have morphed into components of each other, rather than pure systems. According to Merriam-Webster Dictionary, none of these systems actually exist purely anywhere in the world currently. Webster states that socialism is a political theory advocating state ownership of industry or an economic system based on state ownership of capital. Communism is a socialistic scheme of equalizing the social conditions of life; specifically, a scheme which contemplates the abolition of inequalities in the possession of property, as by distributing all wealth equally to all, or by holding all wealth in common for the equal use and advantage of all. Capitalism is an economic system characterized by private or corporate ownership of capital goods, by investments that are determined by private decision, and by prices, production, and the distribution of goods that are determined mainly by competition in a free market.

Even in China, communism in its purest form does not come close to its original definition. China is a political dictatorship that operates as a cross between capitalism and socialism. The rest of the Western countries including Russia and most developing nations are democracies of varying strengths that are hybrids between capitalism and socialism on varying levels. Cuba and North Korea may be the only nations that operate close to communism in its pure since, but Cuba has had to introduce many capitalistic industries into its nation for its survival. North Korea has all but failed economically, and it is in need of constant assistance from other nations to even feed its population.

These systems end up being hybrids of one sort or another because none of these systems in their purist form work. Communism fell by the wayside as a serious alternate economic system to support societies. Capitalism does not exist successfully without a pretty strong dose of socialism, to ensure the benefit of everyone and so that societies don't implode. But even these hybrids have not left us with a clearly sustainable economic system. The most recent global recession demonstrates this point effectively. We need a global economic and monetary system that we control and not one that controls us.

What If There Were No Taxes?

This question provides the basis of the answers to solve many of our problems. If there were no taxes on any level in society (corporate, income, property, sales or any variation), the problems this would cause are easy to delineate. There would be no military, no public safety, and all highways would have to become toll roads. There would be no social safety nets and Social Security and Medicare would disappear. There would be neither regulatory enforcement, nor agencies to check for food, water, environmental, and drug safety. There would be no government at all. Citizen would not pay for government workers or political leaders. This may be welcome from an anarchist perspective, but most people would probably not like it very much. Taxes pay for all these things in our current world and under our current monetary system. Taxes have always been around and came out of taxation by kings and rulers on its citizens to maintain kingdoms. Our taxes today are a carry-over from our previous societies and based on the eventual transformation of monarchies and dictatorships to democratic or representative forms or government. The current taxation system for government revenue has always been in place as a way to raise needed revenues. Therefore, our solutions have always come from within that system.

Essentials of Any Government

In its most basic terms, a government pays for things that are not profitable but needed. These things include services such as schools, trash pick-up, repairing roads, maintaining parks, providing for a military, maintaining infrastructure, and many other oversight and regulatory functions of government.

Taxes are the standard-bearer across the globe in most industrialized countries as a way of funding services to populations. As unpopular as they are, taxes are a necessity to having a functioning industrialized society that provides any level of service to its citizens.

The Problem with Taxes

The anti-tax groups in the United States and abroad are correct about taxations drag on an economy. The basic problem with taxes is that they remove disposable income from households, individuals, and businesses that could otherwise stimulate the economy through increased wages, spending, and investment, which results in business expansion and job growth. When governments grow and spend more money per capita, the ever-increasing tax burden causes the increased removal of disposable income that can create a downward cycle in the economy. Eventually the more taxes that people and business pay, the more that job and wealth creation is slowed, causing the need for increased borrowing and various government-sponsored remedies such as welfare, food stamps, unemployment, and other entitlements. Under our current system part of the government's job is to manage this imbalance to the benefit of society overall.

Taxes, Jobs, and a Living Wage

One cannot have the maximum amount of jobs capitalism can support until the government eliminates the burden of taxes on businesses, individuals, and families, and the government cannot stimulate enough job creation, preferably 100 percent employment, unless there is a living wage that allows everyone to participate in the economy.

The burden of taxes on society can have a negative effect on capitalism by not allowing it to reach its full potential. This is not a new argument and but one that the free market capitalist has espoused for years. The fact is that if the trillions of dollars removed from the wealth of society every year in this country alone were spent as expendable income by businesses, individuals, and families to purchase goods and services, invest and expand business, and increase wages, the stimulation to our capitalistic economy would be tremendous.

On a personal level, a family or individual can spend upwards of 40 to 50 percent of their incomes on taxes and fees of one form or another in many cases. Whether Social Security and Medicare, income (federal, state, county, local), property, or sales taxes, they add up to a large portion of take-home pay. Allowing more expendable income by the removal of taxes from the economic equation and replacing those funds with fiat money would surely mean that people would spend more money on housing, clothes, recreation, and every other good and service, profoundly affecting the economy in a positive manner stimulating expansion of the economy and creating jobs.

A business and or industry no longer paying any taxes (employee, business, property, etc.) would have needed capital to expand their business to support increased demand, hire additional workers, and increase wages. This expansion combined with the expenditure of fiat money by the government through public works and services if necessary would even further cause the economy to grow until 100 percent employment is reached. Currently, and under the current economic theory, 100 percent employment is not a goal of the central banks that control monetary policy. Central banks operate under the economic theory of a "natural rate of unemployment" which means a central bank will actually tighten the money supply by increasing interest rates, when the unemployment rate gets too low, on the posit that wages would increase and inflation would accelerate if they did not. This means that our monetary policies are set up to consciously and proactively keep a certain number of people unemployed. Then we have to turn around and tax society to create safety nets to ensure that those people do not live in abject poverty.

Lastly, a living wage would allow and ensure that people are able to participate in the economy and afford the products and services that capitalism produces. But a living wage without first having jobs has no true impact of society as a whole. The amount of that living wage would vary from nation to nation, state to state, and city to city depending on the cost of living, but is essential to creating stability in the economy. One of the biggest complaints about free market capitalism is that as wage disparities grow, our system becomes increasingly unsustainable. As real wages drop and the middle class is continually squeezed, more and more people cannot afford to participate through travel and purchasing cars, homes, clothing, and other goods and services in the markets which drive our economy.

19 *How to Fix the Future*

When most can only afford to pay for necessities in life our economy will undoubtedly continue to suffer. Figure 3.1 illustrates the wage disparities that have been evident over the last decades within the U.S. and clearly demonstrates that the top 1 percent of earners in the U.S. have steadily received an increasing amount of the income gains over the last few decades to a peak of receiving over 60 percent of the gains in the last ten years.

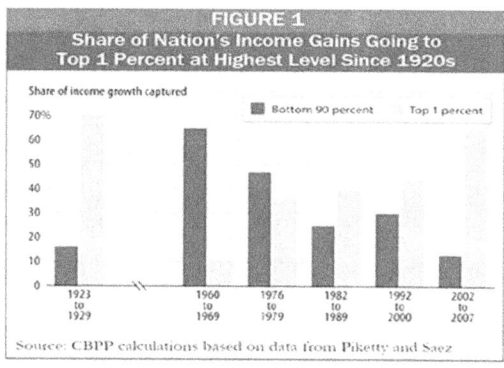

Figure 3.1

Chapter Four

The Myth of Scarcity

Richard Cook said, "Despite the power of industrial processes which have the capability of providing a decent living to everyone in the world—contrary to the myth of global overpopulation—the world still lives under an illusion of scarcity. This tends to justify the senseless struggle for wealth and control of resources. But it's one of the most glaring examples of the condition of mass hypnotism that has weighed humanity down throughout the ages."

Scarcity of land, money, and resources all represent various areas of opinion on shortages that exist in the world today that preclude us from promoting a system where *all* people live under a modern standard of living. In fact, many scarcity proponents would have us believe that we should decrease our standard of living, reduce the population, and acknowledge that some portions of society will always be poor.

There are approximately 5,502,532,127,000,000 square feet of land on the earth. With seven billion people on the earth, that's 786,000 square feet per person. In other words if every person needed 100 square feet to live in, they could all fit in 7 trillion square feet or an area the size of Texas, and that's not even living vertically. This is not to say that population overcrowding is not an issue. Population rates decline when standards of living increase. The key to bending our upward population curve to a sustainable trajectory is to create a fair and equitable global monetary system where everyone participates.

Money, as has been discussed, is a fiat value constantly changing according to the economic situation and monetary policy. It increases and decreases by central banks all the time through adjustments in policy such as, raising or lowering interest rates, and making more capital available to the banking system. There literally is no cap on the amount of money that that society is capable of creating.

Resources, while having a tangible limit, are in basic abundance depending on how we use them. This means that we have untold capabilities to use renewable energy and building technologies to increase the likelihood that we will not exhaust our limited resources when done under a sustainable system.

Chapter Five

Private Money for Public Uses

Why should capitalism's wealth, meaning the sum total of the amount of taxation paid by business and individuals, be required to pay for the desired policies of our government in providing a safety net for the common good of the population? A simple answer is that it is for the good of the nation as a whole. But if an alternative exists, is our current system still the best solution for all involved? Should a business, or for that matter an individual, have to pay for public art or schools if they do not like art or don't have any kids? Should a business have to pay unemployment insurance for people who no longer work for a given company? Should people have to pay for mass transportation if they choose to drive to work or they live in a rural area? The issue is not whether any of these items are necessary or are valuable to society but rather who or what should pay for them.

The current system of taxation and debt creation affects individuals' and businesses' ability to live life and operate business as they see fit. Why should governments take private money to support public policy if an alternative is possible? If we the people want social and physical investments for public use and the common good, we should have the means to pay for it without taking it or borrowing it from private resources.

Unfunded Regulations and Mandates

Anyone who has owned a business or been responsible for implementing federal, state, or local regulations, mandates, and laws is fully aware of the problems and cost associated with implementing new rules that do not come with funding. These regulations and mandates regularly cause businesses to divert profits or cause units of government to institute new levels of taxation to pay for their implementation.

These regulations, laws, and mandates are typically of good reasoning but in more cases than not end up hurting the economy by reducing disposable income from businesses and individuals and indirectly slowing growth.

If these reforms and regulations are good for citizens and are made public will through legislation, then they should come from the public trough. Why can't fiat money pay for regulations? Utilizing fiat money removes the argument made by business owners that regulations, no matter how beneficial to the public, hurt business. If the government of a nation requires an existing company to purchase new scrubbers to lower its emissions or wants car companies to increase gas mileage, it should pay the cost to do so. Regulations, although needed, in a global economy can have profound effects on businesses, especially if another business in another country does not follow the same regulations.

What Could I Buy with My Money?

In a society under our current monetary rules, taxation is a necessary evil to ensure a fair society and to provide for the common good. But under a different system, it holds true and provides a valuable reason why we must debate and consider changing this archaic form of generating national revenue. Reflect a moment on your life and income as an example and compare it to mine. When I was making $60,000 per year, it was astonishing to see how much of that money was left after employment-related taxes, meaning payroll (federal, state, and local), Social Security and Medicare. Out of that $60,000, I ended up taking home around $42,000 after paying all of the taxes. That is $18,000 dollars annually or $1,500 dollars per month of my earned income. I also pay property and sales tax, as well as other fees that raise government revenue and lower my personal wealth.

What could you or I, based on my income at the time, purchase with an additional $1,500 dollars a month. It quickly turns into a quality of life issue for most, a nicer home, a newer car, a family vacation, more trips to my favorite restaurant, tuition at a better school, a college education, or more retirement savings, the list can obviously go on and on.

Whatever the choice may be, the most important thing on a macro and economic level is that those purchases would stimulate the economy and create additional growth within the private sector, not just nationally but globally.

Once you begin to include the other taxes and fees used to support local and state governments that $1,500 dollars per month can easily increase to $3,000 dollars per month.

Those totals usually amount to more than fifty percent of a family or individuals' income. In many European countries, that number is even higher because of their hybrid systems of socialism. The point is that a family that is able to use its income to pay for what it chooses, will have a better quality of life, and will contribute more to the overall economic health and wealth of the its community.

The Military and Taxes

Military spending may be the one appropriate place for taxation, in that it is the one area that does not deserve, nor should it have the unlimited monetary resources that a fiat system can provide. Obviously, if nations can create wealth based on a formula, the expansion and proliferation of various weapons and weapons systems could be a dangerous outcome if left unchecked or if fiat funding goes to military uses. No checks and balances on how much or what to create would be in place, which could lead to a global arms race and careless expansions of military power through fiat money.

For these reasons, military spending should not be a factor in any formula for calculating fiat wealth. If it is included, it should have a strict formula-based need.

Excluding military spending would require nations to tax their citizenry in order to raise funding for military uses. This would serve two main purposes. First, it would control the tendency of nations to build up militaries without the support of their population, and second it would provide for the common defense of nations in a much more democratic fashion because the taxation for military spending would be obvious to those being taxed and would create the necessary checks and balances.

What Happens to National Debt?

The most recent controversy in the United States in the fall of 2011 between the President and Congress over raising the debt ceiling, along with the austerity measures undertaken in some European countries, and the potential default by Greece on its debt during the same time period begs the following questions: what would happen to a nation's existing debt? Since nations and individuals, through bonds and treasury notes, hold the debt, how would it be handled if governments no longer need to tax and borrow money to fund government expenditures?

The simplest solution to the debt questions is to pay debt with fiat money as part of the transition to a global fiat economy. Nations would be required to retire all debt, as debt instruments would relegate to competitive industries only.

Chapter Six

A Global Cooperative Economic System

What would a global Cooperative Economic system look like in practical terms? One perspective is that existing industries, businesses, and government functions become either competitive industries or essential industries. The difference is that competitive industries would be the privately owned for-profit or non-profit businesses or corporations and exist as they do now. For-profit businesses would operate in a more *laissez faire*-type of capitalism; business could operate for truly business motives of profit or advocacy. They could function without having to be concerned with taxation, employee healthcare cost, and unfunded regulations, which can ultimately hurt businesses.

The essential industries would be government-funded and managed and would include most of the traditional responsibilities of government such as police, security, regulatory agencies, and legislative branches.

All citizens would work in either competitive industries or essential industries. Elected officials at the local, state, and national level would be responsible for monitoring both industries, sustaining balance, and planning direction in relation to the needs of society and the goals of the nation, state, or locality.

Essential industries would earn income entirely by the government's fiat money. These government-managed or funded industries would not charge the citizenry for services or goods. They would be free to the public and contain industries and government functions such as: public education, research and development, public transportation, public safety, infrastructure, regulatory agencies, and others functions considered in the national interest. Salaries could range from the minimum wage up to $500,000 per year based on competitive industry wages and industry importance as it relates to society's goals and objectives.

Essential industries would also be the employment backbone for a nation, insuring 100 percent employment and good wages. Government could provide wages to any number of companies or employees to manage, build, and maintain different industries. Some competitive businesses would also receive fiat funding. For instance, a paving company may perform work for competitive industries, but may also perform paving work under government fiat contracts.

Independent countries would control these systems on a national level. The United Nations could control the fiat money formulas, international priorities, and facilitate the standards of transaction and trade between different countries.

Why a Fiat Formula Is Needed?

Central banks and the fractional reserves system create fiat money two ways: the loaning out of money (debt) that does not exist and the printing of money by the central bank as the lender of last resort when needed. This type of system, while allowing for economic growth, also allows for too much money in the system creating the potential for bubbles in the market and inflation. Many would argue that most of this money ends up in the market through increased stock values and business lending. The dot com and housing bubbles, and inflation of the last twenty years demonstrate that when too much money is in the system it has to go somewhere. Whether the extra money goes into dot com businesses that have no demonstrated value or into inflated housing values, that extra money has no relation to the actual needs of a society related to business and industry.

A wealth creation formula is necessary to ensure that the creation of fiat money is flexible and balanced, makes sense for the long-term objectives of a nation, and is in conjunction with a nation's existing capitalistic infrastructure. The goal of the formula should be to ensure competition in the free market, to limit the size and function of government, to ensure that enough money is in the system to have a modern standard of living for all peoples, and to create 100 percent employment.

This might take various forms and include various data points, but in general, first, all participating nations would have to agree upon the formula, more importantly the formula should incorporate a nation's population and expected growth, a nation's minimum standard of living, and the existing capitalistic and public infrastructure that supports a nation's population. In the end the formula should create a fair system of creating fiat money that allows all nations to support their population's basic needs, eliminate the need for borrowing between nations, allow for nations to support their free market capitalistic industries, and allow nations to ensure 100 percent employment of its citizens at a modern standard of living.

Without an agreed upon formula, nations would have the ability to usurp common productive themes of consequential work and fair play. Without a formula to manage the creation of fiat money, a society could become out of balance and inadvertently or purposefully produce a consumption society. Not in the sense of its citizens consuming products and that driving an economy, but in the sense of a large portion of a societies population not working but earning an income through national fiat resources and simply importing all necessary items and services from other societies. It is not hard to imagine a society where the retirement age is forty-five and retirement pay is lavish enough to allow that portion of society to not be a productive part of the global economy, but simply consumers. For this and the other reasons mentioned, a global formula is pertinent for a successful system to emerge.

One possible formula and its components for calculating a nation's annual fiat wealth shows how every nation would calculate its fiat money needs for five or ten-year periods. Fiat wealth would be the final calculation of the amount of fiat money allowed annually to be created by a nation. The current population of a nation is a key component in that it ties fiat wealth to a real tangible figure. Gold backing or the fraction reserve system are based on either the amount of gold you have in your possession or on market indicators that only allow economically developed countries to have a wealth base.

The annual population growth rate (APGR) adds the current population to the estimated population change over one year and divides by the current population. Because this formula requires the amount of wealth needed to support an individual, the growth rate must be determined to account for growth and ensure enough fiat wealth to support a nation's population. Full public cost (FPC) is the amount of money required by a nation to replace all necessary taxation at the local, state, and national levels with the goal of eliminating all taxation on all levels. The national development cost (NDC) is the amount of money required by a nation to develop its public and capitalistic industries, including new infrastructure, training and schools, and safety nets to ensure 100 percent employment. This number is the difference between what a nation's gross domestic product (GDP) should be according to a global modern standard of living index and it current GDP.

The annual per person fiat value (APF) is the per person value generated by adding the full public cost (FPC) and national development cost (NDC) together and dividing by the number of people in the nation (P). The less developed a nation is, the higher this value will be. Using these components the actual formula for first calculating the annual per person fiat value (APF) and then a nation's fiat wealth (FW) could look something like this:

$APF = (NDC + FPC)/P$

$FW = (P + (P * PGR)) * APF$

Chapter Seven

Basic Market Principles

The Inflation Question

Would Cooperative Economics cause runaway inflation? Inflation's root causes are the limitation on the supply of some resource combined with increased demand or too much money in a monetary system that cause wages to rise, triggering an increase in the cost of goods and services. It could be that under a Global Fiat Monetary System the increased purchasing power of citizens and nations would limit or eliminate inflationary pressures first and secondly the fiat wealth formula used in the creation of fiat money would ensure that the amount of fiat money created stays in balance with free market system.

The first limitation on inflationary pressures would come from increased global purchasing of new and improved infrastructure and housing, citizens purchasing their way into modern lifestyles, 100 percent employment, and increased standards of living worldwide. It could reasonably be that if businesses and industries have expanded markets and more revenues, their prices should actually drop, as long as there are sufficient supplies to produce the goods and services desired by the population.

If five billion more people can afford to build a home, pay rent, travel, go to school, buy a computer, shop, and go out to eat, the more money businesses can make to justify lower prices. Similarly, when new products enter a market and market demand increases for the product, eventually prices decrease. It is reasonable to think that sustained economic growth will offset inflationary pressures except in certain cases where there may be an actual limit on the resources necessary to produce a good or service.

In examining the supply side of the argument there are very few actual limitations on the renewable resources needed to build modern societies. There is, or could be, sufficient human, economic, and natural resources available to meet the demand by using available technology currently not in mass use. This may happen when some of the prohibitive cost is out of the equation. For example, solar energy product use subsidized by fiat money in cars, homes, and businesses could occur without the same concern for its economic feasibility. Currently, if I wanted to retrofit all homes, businesses, and industries with solar power, it would be prohibitive on various levels for various reasons ranging from not being able to afford it to not being a good return on the investment. If in calculating the amount of fiat wealth created by a nation, the subsidy required to retrofit all homes, business, and industries to make it economically feasible and show a good return on investment is included in that initial calculation, then that economic barrier disappears.

Second, because the fiat wealth formula takes into account the existing capitalistic infrastructure, capacity, and goals of a nation there is no substantial risk of an oversupply of money that could lead to inflation. This is very different from the system of guesswork that central banks currently undertake. Today central banks decide when to expand or contract money supply based on a variety of economic factors not limited to growth rates, employment rates, inflationary or deflationary indicators, stock markets values, etc. The problem is that many of these things can be counterproductive to what is best for an individual or a business.

Under our system, balance is created, not by having 100 percent employment, but by ensuring there are workers available at competitive wages to industry and business and that inflation (supply and demand) is not caused by increased wages demanded from a non-competitive workforce. If a central bank did not tighten the money supply, the economy would grow too fast and get out of balance. While this makes perfect sense on paper, in practice and to the person that cannot find a job because a central bank tightens credit to slow economic growth, it is no conciliation. It also begs the question of what is the overall goal of our economy and monetary structure as it related to society's goals in the twenty-first century.

In addition only around one-sixth (one billion) of the world's population live in modern societies and most of those do not live at a modern standard of living. Bringing the remaining five to six billion people into a modern standard of living would allow for vast investment opportunities and an expanding economy for decades to come. Those billions of people need work, housing, food, transportation, and clothing. Their children need schools, universities, and doctors and their nations needs clean water, infrastructure, and business investment.

Ultimately, to control inflation several main items are crucial. One is regulating the supply of money in competitive and essential industries by increasing or decreasing the money supply based on the rate of economic growth needed and ensuring balance between the two systems of finance. Two is to disallow the creation of fiat money as a lender of last resort by central banks, regulating closely the reserve rates required by those banks and three, utilizing price ceilings on certain goods and services, if necessary, and subsidies on some goods and services until the system and market are stabilized.

Chapter Eight

The Benefits of a Cooperative Economic System

The benefits of restructuring this system would touch every aspect of life on this planet. Most of the societal problems that we deal with on a daily basis would diminish over time. Problems such as welfare, unemployment, poverty, hunger and starvation, homelessness, various types of crime, and others could disappear from society. If nations had the ability to create their own wealth, they could freely invest in different industries to create jobs by rebuilding housing, infrastructure, and implementing new technologies.

One of the first and most obvious benefits would be the ability to create 100 percent employment worldwide through individual nations. By instituting such changes, 100 percent employment could exist through the economic stimulation of providing higher wages and more disposable income, the creation of or funding of essential industries by the government, and if necessary by adjusting the forty-hour workweek and lowering the retirement age to absorb more employees.

People and businesses would have vast increases in expendable income through increased wages and an elimination of taxes, which would stimulate economies over the globe. This type of system would benefit 99.9 percent of the population, which increases the acceptability of the system to the population. It's difficult to imagine whom it would not benefit in some way.

Other debates such as healthcare and Medicare reform, affirmative action, the deficit, immigration, underfunded education, pollution, and inner-city decline would have no lasting purpose. The elimination of poverty and the negative effects associated with it would diminish. Through 100 percent employment and higher wages many problems that stem from poverty such as hunger, malnutrition, unsanitary and unsafe living conditions, and many forms of crime could be virtually eliminated.

The eventual elimination of pollution and environmental hazards may also be attainable. By giving governments the ability to subsidize the elimination of pollution, industries could no longer use the excuse of improvements not being economically feasible. Governments would have the ability to make environmentally safe practices the law and reverse many current trends that threaten the environment such as rain forest destruction, pollution by fossil fuels, ozone depletion, the greenhouse effect, contamination of our oceans, lakes and streams, and many more.

Governments could fund new technologically-advanced industries throughout the world. Solar and other renewable electric industries could reach their full potential. Advances in transportation through new high-speed railways, new subway systems, as well as new space and aeronautical programs could take place.

An elimination of wars and regional conflicts may also occur if we realize what actually causes these conflicts. These conflicts all relate to money in different ways. Conflicts over land relate to money because in our current system, land equals resources and resources equal money. Other conflicts involve economic oppression. This oppression manifests through race, tribal conflicts, and religion depending on what part of the world you observe. If we remove the limitation on monetary resources then we also, if we choose to, remove the ability (or competitive need) to oppress people who are different from ourselves and we remove the need to fight over land and resources. Much of today's conflicts between groups stems from an imbalance in power and money and the ignorance and reactions that accompany that imbalance. If the circumstances change to eliminate that imbalance, the divisions that have occurred and the reasons for those divisions may disappear.

Restructuring our current system would also spur reforms and changes in many other systems. Our medical research, healthcare, political, judicial, education, and prisons systems would reform. All these systems reflect what is best and fair for society and not what is necessary economically feasible or the status quo.

Through these changes a world with reduced crime, free education and healthcare, little pollution or environmental destruction, no ghettos, bad neighborhoods or poverty and no reason for destructive actions and attitudes, can exist. Time would measure the effects on every field of human activity, which likely would be positive and phenomenal. Other issues influenced by money such as stress, relationships, apathy, self-esteem, jealousy, and ambition would undergo change. These changes would not only affect our own nation, but the entire world we live in, how we perceive it, and our course for the future.

This is not to say that this system would create a purely utopian society. People will always have their flaws of greed, hatefulness, infidelity, anger, just plain crazy, and the list goes on. The question is, how we create the best society we can, not necessarily a perfect one.

Developed vs. Under-developed Countries

The effect on developed vs. under-developed countries depends on what level of development currently exists within the country. The effects on a developing nation like Nigeria and a country like the United States are very different, but both very positive. Let's look at the likely effects on these two countries using some basic economic data.

Nigeria:

2010 Estimated Population:	155,215,573
Gross Domestic Product:	$378 Billion
Per Capita GDP:	$2,422

United States:

2010 Estimated Population:	308,745,538
Gross Domestic Product:	$14.7 Trillion
Per Capita GDP:	$47,123

One of the important factors to first recognize is the comparison in both countries' GDP. The GDP in relation to the per capita GDP gives us an indication of how cooperative economics and a fiat-based system would affect a country. Nigeria's per capita GDP stands at $2,422 dollars compared to the United States $47,123 dollars. This demonstrates that besides having a population with a much higher standard of living, it also reflects the different level of capitalistic infrastructure in each country.

Based on the fiat wealth formula, this means that Nigeria will be allowed to create much more fiat money per capita than the United States, but Nigeria's fiat money would likely go to assist in the funding of banks for starting capitalistic industries and businesses, schools, training, infrastructure that currently do not exist or need vast improvement. Because the United States has a much higher per capita GDP, its needs for fiat money to fill the gap is much lower and would likely go to mainly replace tax revenues. While this would result in positive benefits for both nations,

Nigeria would see a much higher growth rate (than it already has) as it works to absorb its population into a modern standard of living.

The greater the need for development, the more fiat money created based on the fiat wealth formula. This would have the affect of leveling the playing field globally. The eventual outcome being that developing nations would no longer be at the mercy of private outside investment or monetary funds to invest in their countries. They would have the ability to fund their own development and success without the need to borrow money, raise taxes, and surrender development rights to foreign companies.

For a developed country like the United States, it would mean the ability to ensure 100 percent employment, to fix infrastructure, ensure a healthy safety net for seniors and the disabled, along with many other benefits. For under-developed countries like Nigeria, the improvements would likely be more drastic such as new industries to desalinate ocean water and irrigate deserts to grow food, but would also include funding businesses, housing, schools, universities, and cities along with the other items mentioned regarding developed nations.

A Global Modern Standard of Living

One of the largest problems associated with a global market economy and free trade is the imbalance in the standards of living between developed and under-developed nations. The disparity is one of the main reasons that trade agreements can be so devastating to the workers who live in countries like the United States with the higher standards of living. With such a large pool of workers in developing countries willing to work for pennies on the dollar compared to developed nations, it's no wonder the middle class is shrinking and businesses are relocating in order to increase profits.

A global modern standard of living is important for several reasons. Reducing poverty and excessive birthrates, creating demand in the economy, and reducing instability in developing countries are valid reasons that all people should live under a modern standard of living. It also has the ability to make trade agreements more just by removing the incentive for businesses to relocate to low wage nations. A global standard of living should exist in each country through livable minimum wages that are comparable globally to put all nations on a level playing field.

What is a modern standard of living? The answer will depend on whom you ask, but for the purpose of this book, I will assume it to be the ability to afford decent housing, modern conveniences, and the ability to provide for the needs of a family. This amount will differ even within the United States depending on where you live. For instance, the cost of a modern standard of living in New York City is different from the cost of a modern standard of living in Kansas City. But the goal of creating a global wage floor is still the same even if the floor is higher or lower in some areas.

Cooperative Economics and You

As an individual or business owner, what would cooperative economics mean to you? How would it affect your daily life? What would change about how you undertake what we consider our life's journey?

The amount of change seen by an individual or family would be consistent with their location and current economic status. A middle class family living in Columbus, Ohio would be vastly different from a family of five living in Nigeria. But the change would be positive in both cases. If a switch changed our current system to cooperative economics, the family living in Columbus would actually notice little change. Businesses would still open, and the functions of government would remain the same. The biggest differences for the family in Columbus would be an increase in take-home pay because taxes are no longer taken out and having more piece of mind concerning the future. Depending on how and what a government chooses to fund, the family could easily find themselves not having to worry about the cost of college education, medical care, or saving for retirement. They would find it easier to afford to travel, buy that next home, or a new car.

The family in Nigeria would likely see drastic changes. Depending on how the nation decided to implement its planning, the family could see immediate employment and a higher standard of living. The family may see a housing boom that offers them new decent housing and infrastructure improvement where they live. The biggest change for a family in any developing nation would be the ability to support a family in a lifestyle associated with a modern standard of living.

Chapter Nine

The Impacts of a Cooperative Economics System

Public and Private Sector Impact

The benefits of cooperative economics would be far reaching and touch every field of human endeavor in many positive ways. However, as with any change, particularly changes that will directly affect an individuals and or an industry's livelihood, whether it's of overall benefit or not, some may determine the change to be negative. The changes would affect various aspects of public and private sectors in the U.S., as in other nations, by shifts in how we uphold safety nets and set priorities.

One of the largest impacts would concern the public sector in this country. With the benefits associated with cooperative economics, 100 percent employment, living wages, and zero taxes, many public jobs that involve administering assistance programs to the less fortunate or collecting taxes may become obsolete. For instance, housing assistance programs, welfare, and food stamp programs would diminish and those people at the federal and state levels that administrate those types of programs would have to accept different positions in either the public or private sector. The Internal Revenue Service (IRS) would also become obsolete forcing those thousands of workers into different positions. Most change comes easier for some to accept than others do, but with the assurance of 100 percent employment, the reality should be manageable.

Private industries and businesses would likely experience shifts in product and consumer demand. This topic deserves an entire book written on the probable changes to private enterprise based upon the changes to the economic system. For example payday loan or cash advance businesses may not have demand anymore, or energy industries may have to transition to more renewable energies sooner than anticipated because of changes in consumer demand, government regulations, and attitudes.

Rogue Nations

In analyzing the affects of a global fiat system on nations of the world, you cannot ignore the negative effect associated with giving rogue nations a new lease on life. Nations such North Korea and Iran would have the financial ability to maintain their oppressive governments. Dictators, monarchies, and regimes could use fiat resources to prop up their governments by creating enough wealth to support economies, maintain militaries, and suppress opposition.

One solution to this problem could be to only allow nations with true representative governments and free markets to participate in the fiat system. This would effectively create an embargo against nations without representative government and free markets. These nations could try and likely would create their own closed fiat systems with other rouge nations, but nations and their populations would still have a strong incentive to move toward more representative governments and open markets to get the benefits of open trade with the largest economies. Additionally, countries with representative governments and free markets would not have as much of an incentive to do business with rogue nations if they themselves have the ability to invest in infrastructure, and technology that may reduce the need for oil, minerals, or technology that derived from rogue nations.

Chapter Ten

The Big Transition

One of the most frequently asked questions that I receive is, "What would it actually take to implement the system that has been described?" I mentioned briefly about utilizing the United Nation's platform as a vessel for change. While this may be valid, the most difficult aspect of this change would and will be the educational component. People are unknowledgeable about how our monetary system works and the possibilities associated with changing it; informing and convincing the people would be the biggest obstacle. The mechanics are relatively straightforward for changing the system to meet the requirements for cooperative economics. For instance, it could be as relatively simple as nations signing on to a Global Monetary Reform Treaty similar to other global treaties signed in the past, such as Kyoto, Nuclear Non-proliferation, or the Geneva Conventions, except this treaty would require signatory nations to undertake cooperative economic principles and formulas. These items include, but are not limited to:

- Remove the ability of central banks and the banking industry to create money by fiat as the lender of last resort or through the fractional reserve system.
- Agree to debt elimination plans or payback for member nations.
- Agree to calculate individual nations' fiat wealth based upon an agreed fiat formula.
- Maintain a representative form of government.
- Ensure a minimum wage that supports a modern standard of living.
- Eliminate taxation on all levels except for military cost.
- Ensure 100 percent employment for a nation's populace through free markets and government intervention if necessary.
- Ensure that a nation maintains free markets and private property.

That's not to say that these changes would easily pass within member countries once they signed treaties but that is more the aspect of the education of respective citizenships.

Recently on a network news show, a journalist asked Congressman Dennis Kucinich a question about the potential debt ceiling default that was taking place in Congress at the time. His answer was straightforward, but carried a clue to what needs to occur not only in this country, but also in parliaments and governmental bodies across the globe.

Congressman Kucinich stated: "You know, Ed, I carry the Constitution with me. I want to tell you something. We shouldn't have to get to that. But Congress ought to familiarize itself with Article One, Section Eight, which says the Congress has the power to borrow money, sure, but it also has the power to coin money, to make money. We gave that power over to the Federal Reserve back in 1913. It's time that we understood we don't have to go to banks to get money. The United States is a sovereign government. According to our Constitution, we should be able to invest in our own people, create the jobs. We shouldn't have to rely on banks. We cannot be at the mercy of banks in this country. That's not a democracy. I think that it's time the Congress studied that provision of the Constitution as well."

There is no big transition to discuss as yet, only the need and desire to bring to light the possibility of change. To push that possibility into debate across the globe into homes, businesses, media, and classrooms and to be willing to think outside of the box and do what is best for everyone on earth as we move into this next millennium and figure out how to fix the future.

www.ingramcontent.com/pod-product-compliance
Lightning Source LLC
Chambersburg PA
CBHW070428180526
45158CB00017B/921